# COMFORTABLE CHRISTIANITY
## GROUP STUDY

# INTRODUCTION

Dear readers,

I formed this study guide to facilitate an edifying group discussion. For several years, the Bible study at my church seemed pointless. After reading a Bible passage, we would go through it verse-by-verse, asking people what stood out or what they learned from it. There wasn't a clear moderator, and the conversations would get off on a tangent. I stopped going, as did many others. Ultimately, the Bible study fizzled out.

Years later, while writing *Comfortable Christianity*, my church asked me to lead a Bible study. I was reluctant to come back, remembering how pointless it had seemed before. But this time, we employed some tactics that we found were effective, engaging, and kept us on topic. I want to help you re-create that kind of an environment with your youth group/book club/Bible study.

Each chapter has a quick summary, a key verse, and discussion questions. I encourage you to select someone to moderate the discussion—ideally someone who likes to get others involved instead of talking him/herself the whole time. Moderators should also familiarize themselves with the questions in advance. You can cover several chapters each session based on your group's size and desired pace. Finally, I encourage you to finish each discussion with a prayer, addressing the issues that were brought up.

I hope my openness allows you to be transparent as well, because we need to encourage and keep one another accountable. My prayer is that this book and group study guide will strengthen you and your group.

Sincerely,

Caleb Seifu

"May God deliver us from the easygoing, smooth, comfortable Christianity that never lets the truth get a hold of us." -A.W. Tozer

# YOU'RE GOING TO HELL, BRO & PRELUDE

**KEY VERSE:** "Examine yourselves to see if your faith is genuine." 2 Corinthians 13:5

1. Considering the possibility of people being cast into hell, what is the main reason that we don't tell them about Jesus?
2. Have you ever considered the possibility of going to hell despite considering yourself a Christian?
3. Is it peculiar that "my bartender" was grouped in the list of people who are going to hell? Elaborate.
4. What is the importance of examining your faith regularly? Do you do it? Elaborate.

Ask if anyone has any additional thoughts before closing.

# CHAPTER 1: THE HANGOVER

I begin the book in a youth retreat setting. When placed in an environment where your peers are all believers, it is easy to focus on Christ. The problem arises when the camp is over and everyone returns to the real world.

After being greatly moved at camp, only to fizzle out afterward, I decided it was best to not allow God to move me as much next camp. In essence, I built a greater tolerance against the conviction of the Spirit with each camp.

I made a conscious decision not to be on fire for God (like many of my friends), nor abandon my faith and become a total rebel—I decided to follow Jesus from afar and live in a state of perpetual lukewarm-ness.

**KEY VERSE:** "I am sending you out like sheep among wolves. Therefore be as shrewd as snakes and as innocent as doves." Matthew 10:16

1. Have you ever attended a Christian retreat or camp? If so, did you go for God, for fun, or for a potential husband/wife?
2. What was your retreat or camp experience like? Did it seem to be an emotional rollercoaster in the end, or did you manage to gain and maintain something?
3. The author calls time for God simple economics of supply and demand. At a retreat, there is a lot of time for prayer and reflection, but once we go back to the real world, it becomes difficult to give God any time at all. Why? Is being too busy a valid excuse?
4. What are some things that we should technically be too busy to do, but we find time anyway?

5. Have you ever intentionally refused to allow the Holy Spirit to move you? Why?
6. In the section *Wolf Pack Demographics*, I note how different the early church is from the modern church. In what ways have we deviated/compromised?
7. Do we take comfort in knowing that other Christians are also deviating/compromising? Why?
8. What does it mean to follow Jesus from afar? Why do we do it? Is there comfort in thinking you are still 'following'?

Ask if anyone has any additional thoughts before closing.

# CHAPTER 2: PASSION OF THE CHRISTIAN

In this chapter, I refer to my desire to associate myself with Christ while suppressing the thought of His sacrifice. Otherwise, it would be difficult to continue my lukewarm lifestyle.

In the section, *The Masquerade Ball*, I address the prosperity gospel—the wolves and their followings. "If we have material motives, (for seeking God) we become like Judas. Just as he sealed the betrayal with a kiss, we seal our betrayal with the public appearance that we love Jesus. (We really love money)."

Then finally in, *Luke(warm) I Am Not Your Father*, I discuss how easy it is to become lukewarm despite once having passion for God. All we have to do is let the passion cool and conform to our surrounding.

**KEY VERSE:** "Then Jesus answered, 'Will you really lay down your life for me? Very truly I tell you, before the rooster crows, you will disown me three times!'" John 13:38

1. Do you get emotional/choked up when watching movies like *Passion of the Christ?* Do those emotions last/turn into something (repentance), or just fade away?
2. Do you suppress the thought of Christ's sacrifice in order to compromise in an area of your faith? Elaborate.
3. It is very popular to call oneself a 'work in progress.' Although this is true, can it become a counterintuitive mindset—enabling sin and compromise?
4. The author notes that he would toss $20 into the offering bucket to ease his mind. Why is making a superficial appearance before other believers so important to us?
5. Is tithing a command for today's Christians, or is it taken out of context?

6. What would the early church/apostles think of the prosperity gospel? Has it tarnished Christianity's public image? If so, how?
7. What are your thoughts on being 'slain in the spirit'?
8. What causes us to lose our zeal for Christ? What can we do to maintain it, or revive it?
9. Peter wanted to prove his loyalty attacking a Roman soldier. Why is it easier to fight for Jesus than give ourselves up?
10. Why do we see non-violence as weakness even though it takes more strength?
11. The author asks if our faith hurts or heals our enemies. Has your faith ever healed an enemy?

Ask if anyone has any additional thoughts before closing.

# CHAPTER 3: THE ENCOUNTER

In this chapter, I discuss how the true enemies of God are not angry atheists, but rather, Comfortable Christians, specifically those who use God to endorse their position. Christians have become the cause by which "the name of God is blasphemed" (Romans 2:24).

I also talk about fear-based faith, and how it has been used to scare people into belief. This tactic doesn't help motivate people to become like Christ, but rather do just enough to avoid damnation.

Finally, the chapter reflects on being the light of the world. We often consider non-believers as blind—people who need guidance. However, we often allow God's light to dim—sometimes to the point where we too are walking in darkness. Ultimately, our encounter with Christianity may be based on religious fear, tradition, or social comfort.

**KEY VERSE:** "If you were blind, you would not be guilty of sin; but now that you claim you can see, your guilt remains." John 9:41

1. Are you irritated/angered by atheists? Elaborate.
2. Why is being lukewarm like being an enemy of God?
3. What does it mean to use God to endorse your position? Can you think of any examples of where that is being done in public? How does it hurt Christianity?
4. Have you ever allowed the God's conviction/presence within you to dim? When and why?
5. When we become obedient, we tend to think of ourselves as good. But Jesus said being able to see would mean our guilt remains—God will always have more to work on us if we allow Him to. Are there things in our life that we don't allow His light to penetrate? What and why?

6. The Pharisees thought they were the closest to God, but they were the furthest. In what ways can we fall into that same trap?

7. Discuss Matthew 6:22-23: "The eye is the lamp of the body. If your eyes are healthy, your whole body will be full of light. But if your eyes are unhealthy, your whole body will be full of darkness. If then the light within you is darkness, how great is that darkness!" How does it relate to our society today?

8. Have you lost passion/purpose for seeking Christ? In what ways?

Ask if anyone has any additional thoughts before closing.

# ATHEISTS & CHRISTIANS UNITE

1. Atheists often write incendiary comments online. Have you ever found yourself so angry that you were fighting, maybe even cursing at them? How does that defeat your purpose?
2. What is the letter trying to convey about Christian discipline?
3. What weakness does the letter point out that you may be experiencing? What have you done or what will you do with the knowledge of these problem areas?
4. The letter brings up many things atheists and comfortable Christians have in common, including that they both consider themselves to be 'good people.' Why is this a problem?
5. What group—atheists or Christians—is the real loser of this proposal? Why?

Ask if anyone has any additional thoughts before closing.

# CHAPTER 4: I DREAM OF JESUS

This chapter begins with an analogy in which our relationship with God is likened to a homeless man begging for money—not to get food, but to use it at his discretion. Often times, we may be praying for non-essentials and/or things that may harm us.

I discuss three types of farce prayers—1) either made in lieu of being responsible, 2) contradicting God's nature, and 3) a verbatim prayer. I realize that these prayers are purely selfish. They all have to do with my desires and concerns—ultimately, treating Jesus like a genie.

I encourage you to examine whether you are part of either the Lord's entourage or paparazzi—we're either in the crowd trying to receive from Him, or in the inner circle becoming His extensions.

**KEY VERSE:** "When you ask, you do not receive, because you ask with wrong motives, that you may spend what you get on your pleasures." James 4:3

1. Discuss the 3 types of 'farce prayers': those made in lieu of being responsible, those that contradict God's nature, and verbatim prayers. Which kind do you make the most? Give an example.
2. What are some of the ridiculous requests you have prayed for? Do you realize they are ridiculous or could even hurt you at the time you're praying them? Why/why not?
3. What do you believe God thinks of our wishful prayers?
4. In the section, *To Pray or Not to Pray*, the author talks about how he is, in essence, trying to bribe God. Have you ever tried to bribe God? Did you keep your promise?
5. Discuss John 14:13: "And I will do whatever you ask in my name, so that the Father may be glorified in the Son."

What do the things we pray for tell us about who or what we really glorify?"

6. What is the danger of routine verbatim prayers?
7. Do you say the Lord's Prayer? If not, why? If so, how do you ensure it doesn't become a verbatim prayer?
8. Do you find it difficult to pray for longer than 5 minutes? Why?
9. How does praying for others affect you?
10. Discuss Matthew 13:11: "He replied, 'Because the knowledge of the secrets of the kingdom of heaven has been given to you, but not to them.'" What is the difference between the 'yous' and the 'thems,' and how do you know which group you're in?
11. Why is being Jesus's paparazzi a problem for Christianity?

Ask if anyone has any additional thoughts before closing.

# CHAPTER 5: GOD IS GOOD, SOMETIMES

I begin this chapter disgruntled with the liberal use of the phrase, 'God is good'--especially after one receives some non-essential, material thing. I tried to split the difference between a coincidence and God's miraculous favor.

I came across a journal from my youth, which was filled with incredibly depressing material. After losing my brother to cancer, faith and purpose felt meaningless. But then, I got into a relationship with a friend who had lost her father to cancer, and the cloud of depression left me—temporarily. When that relationship ended, my depression resurfaced, and this time it was worse.

The chapter grows darker and more skeptical about whether we would say, "God is good" when terrible things happen. Then I discuss an article about a survivor of human trafficking who had seen and endured unconscionable pain. The survivor told the interviewer to tell anyone else who has survived this, "Let the strength of Job be with you."

We often forget that the cross doesn't symbolize comfort; it symbolizes suffering and redemption. We often depend on God to spare us pain as opposed to 1) giving us the strength to push through, and 2) using our pain to relate and help others going through similar hurt.

**KEY VERSE:** "My God, my God, why have you forsaken me? Why are you so far from saving me, so far from my cries of anguish?" Psalm 22:1

1. Do people who give God thanks for things like green lights and parking spots upset you, or are you one of those people?
2. Do we give God as much praise in the bad times as we do in the good? Why is it important to give praise in bad times?

3. Have you or are you going through a time of depression and/or purposelessness? If so, was it induced by something, or did it just creep in?
4. If you have overcome depression and purposelessness, how did you get through it? What practical advice or prayer would you give to others who are currently going through it?
5. Have you ever tired to overcome depression the wrong way? How did it affect you?
6. Have you been, or are you currently mad at God? Why?
7. What practical advice or prayer would you give to others who are currently upset with God?
8. In what ways can suffering either lead you to the cross, or away from the cross?
9. Have you ever found strength or encouragement in the story of Job, the way the survivor of the human trafficking had?
10. Do we sometimes forget that God's plan isn't comfortable, and that the cross means suffering?
11. In what ways can we help or relate to people going through similar suffering?
12. Discuss Matthew 11:28-29: "Come to me, all you who are weary and burdened, and I will give you rest. Take my yoke upon you and learn from me, for I am gentle and humble in heart, and you will find rest for your souls." Why is it practical or how has it been practical to you?

Ask if anyone has any additional thoughts before closing.

## MERLOT OR MEDICINE

1.  Have you ever gone on WebMD and convinced yourself you are dying? What disease did you think you had?
2.  Have you ever tried to find scriptural justification for something you wanted to be right? Elaborate.
3.  Who is your 'my Jesus,' and is He a figment of your imagination?
4.  People often us the phrase, "God knows my heart" to settle a contradiction? Why is that dangerous or self-deceptive?
5.  Discuss the following quote:

*"We have all departed from that total plan in different ways, and each of us wants to make out that his own modification of the original plan is the plan itself. You will find this again and again about anything that is really Christian: every one is attracted by bits of it and wants to pick out those bits and leave the rest. That is why we do not get much further: and that is why people who are fighting for quite opposite things can both say they are fighting for Christianity."* -C. S. Lewis

How does this hurt Christians as a whole? In what ways are we guilty?

Ask if anyone has any additional thoughts before closing.

# CHAPTER 6: AMBIGIOUS ALMIGHTY

This chapter begins exploring how Jesus has been portrayed in terms of physical attributes. We obviously want our Savior to be tall, strong, and handsome. Some of us may even want him to appear like us racially. But beyond the trivial physical misrepresentations are the more serious and dangerous, ideological misrepresentations. We want Jesus to support the same things we support—whether they be political, prosperity driven, etc.

Instead of representing Jesus, we create a Jesus that represents us—and by default, a Jesus who opposes who we oppose. Ultimately, we turn people away from the real Jesus because of our representation of Him.

We don't like to think of ourselves as turning people away from Jesus, but how many people have we actually led to Him? If we're living compromising lives, we like to think we have neutral influence. But if our friends and co-workers know that we are Christian, they will examine our lives, even if we don't.

**KEY VERSE:** "You are the salt of the earth. But if the salt loses saltiness, how can it be made salty again? It is no longer good for anything, except to be thrown out and trampled underfoot." Matthew 5:13

1. Do you ever get into heated disputes about Jesus's race? Is Jesus going to love you more because you are His skin color? How can obsessing about Jesus's race be harmful or distracting?
2. What are some ideological misrepresentations or doctrines within Christianity? Why are they dangerous?
3. Why is it so difficult not to judge people on 'outward appearance'?
4. In the section, *Skeleton in the Closet*, the author likens being a Christian to being a foreigner. In what ways is this true?

5.  Do you tell your friends and co-workers about Jesus? Why or why not? Have you ever done so while being intoxicated or buzzed?
6.  Would it be better for 'Christianity' if your friends/co-workers didn't know you were a Christian? Why?
7.  Discuss Matthew 5:13 (above). Have you ever been, or are you currently 'salt that has lost your saltiness'?

Ask if anyone has any additional thoughts before closing.

# CHAPTER 7: PLATFORM POLITICS

This chapter begins with a quote from Kevin Durant's MVP (Most Valuable Player) award speech—saying that basketball is just a platform for Jesus. God has given us all a platform, but we often overlook look its importance and responsibilities. We may want God to expand our platform, whether through a better job or position, and we promise to give Him praise in it. Oftentimes, we promise to be faithful with more even though we haven't been faithful with less.

Throughout history, people have used God as a platform for their own agendas, oftentimes to support their self-righteousness, status, and profit.

Ultimately, we should be careful that our current platform, however small or insignificant we think it is, doesn't take glory away from God.

**KEY VERSE:** "Let your light shine before men in such a way that they may see your good works, and glorify your Father who is in heaven." Matthew 5:16

1. Who's your favorite Christian celebrity? Why?
2. Why do we love to see celebrities giving glory to God?
3. Do Christian celebrities validate us somehow? If so, why?
4. Do you consider your platform to give God glory as insignificant? Have you been faithful with it? If so, give examples.
5. Why is it easy to think that you could give glory to God on a larger platform even though you haven't on a small platform?
6. How much impact does a celebrity make on unbelievers by glorifying God on TV? Compare that to how much impact a normal person makes on unbelievers by living in a way that glorifies God.

7. Give examples of how people use 'God' to support their personal positions or ambitions. How does this affect others?
8. Has mainstream Christianity become like the temple Jesus overthrew with a whip? Elaborate.
9. Who is today's Barabbas? What does the author mean when he asks, "Have you ever wondered if you were a follower of Barabbas, and not Jesus?"

Ask if anyone has any additional thoughts before closing.

# CHAPTER 8: JESUS PIECE

In this chapter, I discuss how we may not be ashamed claiming of Jesus; at times, it may even be trendy to do so. Christian or not, many people love the idea of Jesus—granted, it's their own personal view of Him.

During Jesus's ministry, there was much debate about who He was. That debate continues today. If we believe Him to be the Son of God, then our testimony must not only be verbal, but also through our actions. In fact, by claiming to know Him despite producing the evidence of that in action, we further blur people's understanding.

Just as the disciples were overly concerned about which of them would be the greatest, we often concern ourselves too much about where we stand, or what our grand purpose is. Jesus taught His disciples by example, that being great meant humbly serving.

**KEY VERSE:** "Be careful not to practice your righteousness in front of others to be seen by them. If you do, you will have no reward from your Father in heaven. So when you give to the needy, do not announce it with trumpets, as the hypocrites do in the synagogues and on the streets, to be honored by others." Matthew 6:1-2

1. What is so funny or ridiculous about rappers giving glory to God?
2. Have you, or someone you know ever represented Jesus with clothes or accessories, while simultaneously opposing Him in action?
3. Has an unbeliever ever told you a negative story about what a 'Christian' said or did that turned them off to Christianity? What was your response?
4. At the end of the section *Who Is Jesus Really*, is the author telling people not to witness unless they are perfect? How

does this section practically apply to our lives being a testimony?

5. What is our definition of being a great person compared to God's definition of greatness?

6. Is it comforting or helpful that Jesus exemplified humility instead of just demanding it?

7. How would you react if Jesus washed your feet? Would you be disturbed, like Peter? If so, why?

8. Do you consider yourself to be a humble person? Why or why not?

9. Discuss Matthew 6:1-2 (key verse). Why do we feel the need to be validated when we're serving?

Ask if anyone has any additional thoughts before closing.

# CHAPTER 9: THE FIRST STONE

I begin this chapter by expressing my displeasure with a close friend who positively criticized me for negatively criticizing a secular music group. I was sure that I had a justifiable stance to judge—a stance that hinged on the fact that the music group was a worse hypocrite than I was.

Oftentimes, when someone is caught in some sin, we not only judge them, but we also use Jesus to judge them—just like the Pharisees tried to do with the woman caught in adultery. We often assume that 1) someone else's sin is worse than ours, 2) attack sin/sinners selectively, 3) envision Jesus condemning them.

Everyone complains about judgmental people, but we often forget how judgmental we can be ourselves. Like the author, we too may feel that we are 'surrounded by savages'... looking at everyone's faults, but never our own.

In the section, *Compare and Condemn*, the author reflects on a chapter about pride in C.S. Lewis's book *Mere Christianity*. Pride is the worst sin, yet it sneaks its way into the core of Christian behavior. It can actually be used to defeat other sins! Lewis states, Satan "is perfectly content to see you becoming chaste and brave and self-controlled provided, all the time, he is setting up in you the Dictatorship of Pride."

**KEY VERSE:** "Search me, God, and know my heart; test me and know my anxious thoughts. See if there is any offensive way in me, and lead me in the way everlasting." Psalms 139:23-24

1. Many people think they can take positive criticism well. Share a time when you did not take it well, or someone did not take your positive criticism well.
2. Why is it so hard to accept positive criticism? How does it prevent us from keeping one another accountable?

3.  Is it wrong to overlook something in fear of a backlash? What steps can you take to give better, more acceptable criticism or accountability?

4.  Share a time you caught yourself judging someone. How did you correct yourself?

5.  What does the author say is 'all it takes' to judge someone? Have you ever been shocked by how much you judge?

6.  Do modern day Pharisees realize they are modern day Pharisees? Why or why not?

7.  Discuss the section, *Surrounded by Savages*. Do we feel like we are surrounded by savages? If so, how does that hurt our ability to reach people with the Gospel?

8.  Why is pride so dangerous?

9.  Have you ever beat a sin with pride (like Lewis mentioned)? For example, "I'm a real Christian; I'm not going to get drunk with you heathens."

10. Discuss the opening quote in section *Compare and Condemn*. How can you fall into this danger?

11. What is the first step towards humility? (answer: the realization that we are proud)

Ask if anyone has any additional thoughts before closing.

## CHAPTER 10: THE LAST STONE

This chapter addresses a hot-button issue—homosexuality. I assume that many readers, like me, are evolving on their approach to homosexuals. I noted that our gradual acceptance of the gay community is mostly due to the media, but claims that the church should have been the first to accept them, not the last (the people themselves, not the sexual practice).

I don't attempt to solve the problem of homosexuality in the church, but rather the way we go about the problem. Is hate for homosexuality sex due to a genuine hate of sin, or a selective hate of a certain type of sin?

Ultimately, I admit that the issue is not for me to champion, but rather people who have either overcome sexual orientation or have chosen (gulp) celibacy. Remember, Paul boasted in his weakness. It's weakness that relates; it's weakness that reaches.

As much as I sympathize for gay believers, I cannot in good conscience advocate homosexual sex. In addition, I am reminded of the Apostle Paul's warning, "For the time will come when people will not put up with sound doctrine. Instead, to suit their own desires, they will gather around them a great number of teachers to say what their itching ears want to hear." 2 Timothy 4:3

America is often depicted as a Christian nation going through moral decay. But in reality, society never really represented Christianity; on the contrary, society made Christianity represent it. The country's faith was superficial, yet it is that superficiality that we are trying desperately to maintain.

**KEY VERSE:** "For the time will come when people will not put up with sound doctrine. Instead, to suit their own desires, they will gather around them a great number of teachers to say what their itching ears want to hear." 2 Timothy 4:3

1. Were you ever homophobic? Elaborate.
2. Do you have gay friends? If so, what are their thoughts on faith?
3. How would things have been different if the church had spearheaded tolerance before the media did?
4. How would you respond if a close member of your family came out as gay? Would it change your beliefs?
5. Why have believers who identify as gay but choose to be abstinent become targets for the world? In what ways can we support these believers?
6. There are teachers who interpret the Bible in ways that accept homosexual marriage. Discuss why/how this kind of teaching can be attractive to gay believers.
7. Discuss 2 Timothy 4:3 (key verse).
8. Discuss Matthew 21:31: "Jesus said to them, 'Truly I tell you, the tax collectors and the prostitutes are entering the kingdom of God ahead of you.'" How does it apply to us?
9. The author talks about how his parents, who emigrated from Ethiopia (in the 1980's), were shocked by racism in America, even in the church. Historically, why was it so difficult for people of faith to accept people of color?
10. Why do we bemoan 'moral decay' if morals don't save souls? Why are we so desperate for social morality to resemble Christian morality?
11. Discuss Matthew 23:25-26: "Woe to you, teachers of the law and Pharisees, you hypocrites! You clean the outside of the cup and dish, but inside they are full of greed and self-indulgence. Blind Pharisee! First clean the inside of the cup and dish, and then the outside also will be clean." How does it relate to the country and to us personally?

Ask if anyone has any additional thoughts before closing.

# CHAPTER 11: LOVE: THY NEIGHBOR

In this section, I begin by sharing a story about street ministry gone wrong! I went with my church to skid row, assuming that those who have hit rock bottom would surely be receptive to Jesus. But the homeless weren't very welcoming, and seemed to be familiar or irritated with people coming in church groups.

I also talked about how our churches have become like clubs. In fact, I continued going to my church mainly because of the cultural reciprocity. I even admitted my hesitance to accept people who were not of my nationality.

In the section, *Keep Your Friends Close, Your Enemies Closer*, I talked about responding to hate with love and what affect that has on people. Our faith is meaningless unless it is accompanied with love.

Paul did everything he could to relate, for the sake of spreading the Gospel. We don't care that much though. Sure, we may not hate our neighbor, but we're oftentimes indifferent—which is actually worse.

**KEY VERSE:** "If you love those who love you, what reward will you get? Are not even the tax collectors doing that? And if you greet only your own people, what are you doing more than others? Do not even pagans do that?" Matthew 5:46-47

1. Have you ever done street ministry? Tell us about your experience. Were people receptive to you?
2. If the people you ministered to on the street, came to your church, would they feel accepted?
3. Have you ever gone to a church that was not primarily your racial makeup? Did you feel welcomed or awkward?
4. What are the benefits or downfalls of having a church comprised of your own race and nationality?

5. Discuss James A. Baldwin's quote, "Nobody is more dangerous than he who imagines himself pure in heart; for his purity, by definition, is unassailable."

6. People can make us so angry. How may lashing out at them affect their view of Christianity?

7. Why is it so difficult to value people the way God values them? Discuss what it would mean to be 'not a respecter of persons.'

8. Why do we value the rich and celebrities so much? Does it have to do with our desire to be like them?

9. How can we, like Paul, be all things to all people in order to spread the gospel? Do you have an example of sharing the Gospel with someone who was not like you in race, age, etc.?

Ask if anyone has any additional thoughts before closing.

# CHAPTER 12: LOVE: CHASIN' FEELINGS

I begin this chapter talking about relationships and the feeling of love as opposed to the action of love. There are similarities with our relationship with God—it may only be based on our feelings.

Worship music can cause us to feel a certain way, and we may deceive ourselves into thinking that we are truly worshipping when we may just be on an emotional high. Oftentimes, the promises we make in the songs are no more than lip service. In reality, we worship what consumes our thoughts, desires, and devotion.

If our love for Jesus is based on feelings or emotions, it may not last. Ultimately, we may be looking for the benefits of a relationship with Christ, without actually committing.

**KEY VERSE:** "These people honor me with their lips, but their hearts are far from me. They worship me in vain; their teachings are merely human rules." Matthew 15:8-9

1. Why is the 'feeling' of love so important to us? How can it be deceiving?
2. Do you see love as a responsibility? Does that perspective take the romance out of it?
3. Is our relationship with God—our love for Him—contingent or how we're feeling? How does that play out in your daily life?
4. Have you ever been caught up in the emotion of worship? Is that true worship?
5. Discuss the CC guy's questions ("It may seem ideal to feel God's presence all the time, but what about on Saturday night? Do you really want to feel His presence on the dance floor? Or when you're in bed with your boyfriend/girlfriend?"). It may seem ideal to always feel

God's presence, but what are some compromising situations you engage in, in which you wouldn't want to feel His presence?

6. Discuss the relationship dynamic in the section *Backstage Passes*. How does this relate to you?

7. What in your life is competing with God for your worship? What consumes your thoughts, desires, and devotion?

8. Have you ever received lip service? How did you react to it?

9. Have you ever given lip service to God? Elaborate.

10. The section, '*What are we?*' discusses the concept of being a non-committed Christian. Are you in a relationship with Jesus, or are you just dating Him? How long have you been dating? What is preventing you from committing?

Ask if anyone has any additional thoughts before closing.

# CHAPTER 13: LOVE: THY GOD

In this chapter, I discuss what it means to love God in the way Jesus taught us to—with all of our heart, mind, strength, and soul.

When we're trying so hard to obey God, instead of loving what God loves, we may find ourselves either breaking character or breaking up.

The section *Hearts and Minds* draws similarities between a military occupation and trying to maintain faith when your heart doesn't belong to God. 'Freedom in Christ' is not freedom to someone who wants to continue living in sin. If we don't agree with God's definition of freedom, then trying to maintain our faith leads to inner turmoil and conflict.

Also, the strength of our love for God will be tested, and it won't stand a chance without strict training.

**KEY VERSE:** "Put to death, therefore, whatever belongs to your earthly nature: sexual immorality, impurity, lust, evil desires and greed, which is idolatry." Colossians 3:5

1. Have you ever considered a boyfriend or girlfriend to be your soulmate, only to realize later that it was only infatuation? Why was it so hard to see that while you were in the relationship? What can you do to avoid it in the future?
2. Are the fruits of the Spirit in your life being produced as a result of your relationship with God, or are you forcing it? Give examples.
3. Discuss what it means for God to "create in you a new heart." Is that a regular prayer of yours?
4. What is the key to overthrowing our greatest adversary— the flesh? (Answer: Meditating on the Word)

5. David says, "Oh, how I love your law! I meditate on it all day long." Does that seem enjoyable, or is it a task?

6. The author talks about meditating on Tupac lyrics—he could never get sick of Tupac. What are some things or someone that you meditate on all day?

7. Do you ever try to 'spot train' certain sins away? What can we do to resolve spiritual problem areas?

8. The author reflected on how he may never be spiritually mature enough to 'turn the other cheek'. Do you ever set limits on potential spiritual growth? Elaborate.

9. Are you on spiritual life support? (loving God with only your heart, but not your mind, strength, and soul). How do you know if your response to wake up isn't simply an 'automatic behavior'?

Ask if anyone has any additional thoughts before closing.

# CHAPTER 14: THE GREAT OMISSION

In this chapter, I share about how my desire to help the needy (as a child) turned into a disdain of them. In a big city like Los Angeles, it's easy to get accustomed and even irritated by the homeless, prostitutes, etc. However, Christ's love extended to those who were outcasts and rejected—consider His interactions the Samaritan woman, the prostitute washing his feet, the prostitute about to be stoned, lepers, etc.

In the section *Bad Religion*, I discuss how Jesus calls the converts of Pharisees "twice as much a child of hell as you are." The section also touches a time when gentile converts were being addressed regarding the rules/laws of the Torah (Acts 15:29).

The section *The Interpreter* talks about Scripture that is taken out of context—usually in order to back a personal agenda. Ultimately, the very element that gets omitted from Christianity is the one necessary for it to be meaningful—love.

**KEY VERSE:** "If I speak in the tongues of men or of angels, but do not have love, I am only a resounding gong or a clanging cymbal." 1 Corinthians 13:1

1. In your younger days, did you want to serve God? What about now? If not, what happened?
2. Why is it easy to grow cold toward society's outcasts?
3. Does the fact that Jesus 'ate with sinners' mean that we can be in environments of sin too? Where do we draw the line?
4. What does it mean to "strain out a gnat and swallow a camel?" In what ways are we guilty of this?
5. What laws do you believe a Christian must follow or does not have to follow from the Old Testament and why? What is your interpretation based on?

6. Discuss Acts 15:29: "You are to abstain from food sacrificed to idols, from blood, from the meat of strangled animals and from sexual immorality. You will do well to avoid these things. Farewell." Why was this council's letter to Gentile believers (beginning with verse 22) and the entire chapter so monumental regarding keeping the law?
7. What common verses do people often take out of context? How are they harmful?
8. Are there any verses that you have taken out of context? How were you corrected?
9. Discuss 1 Corinthians 13:1 (key verse).
10. How has practicing Christianity without Christ's love tainted the Gospel, both historically and presently?

Ask if anyone has any additional thoughts before closing.

# CHAPTER 15: THE BROAD OF CHRIST

This chapter begins by discussing Hosea, a prophet who was commanded to marry a prostitute as an example of God's relationship with us. Christians are called to be the Bride of Christ, yet the fruits that many of us bear are not of Him. This ultimately brings shame and mockery from the people who see Christians as hypocrites.

Often times, we produce fruits that are good and bad... we rationalize that it's okay or we're not perfect. Instead of confronting our faults, we oftentimes think of the good things we've done. But Jesus told us to abide in Him so that we would bear His fruit. Ultimately, the reason we are producing fruits of the flesh is because part of us is still abiding in the world.

**KEY VERSE:** "By their fruit you will recognize them. Do people pick grapes from thorn bushes, or figs from thistles? Likewise, every good tree bears good fruit, but a bad tree bears bad fruit." Matthew 7:16-17

1. How would you respond if God told you to marry a prostitute?
2. Would you be able to love someone who was not committed to you? If not, why does God love us?
3. What fruits of the Spirit are lacking in our lives? Why?
4. Why is it so difficult to abide in Jesus consistently? Is your answer an excuse?

Ask if anyone has any additional thoughts before closing.

# CHAPTER 16: THE CASE FOR COMPROMISE

This chapter is written by the alter ego, who is always looking for ways to compromise, yet stay a Christian. He seeks to modify the Bible for current times, and his first aim is at Paul's "outdated" letter to be vigilant in regards to spiritual warfare. He goes in depth about his desire to stay off of the devil's radar, even if it means missing God's full purpose for him.

Ultimately, he advises us to continue compromising and gives tips on how to rationalize gray areas.

**KEY VERSE:** "It's not what goes into a man that defiles him, but what comes out" (Matthew 15:11).

1. Do you give any thought to the spiritual battle around you, or do you ignore it?
2. How does ignoring spiritual warfare work to the devil's advantage?
3. Have you ever encountered spiritual opposition/hardship when you were walking in God's plan like Nehemiah? Elaborate.
4. What are some gray areas that you excuse even though they are spiritually detrimental?
5. Are there some gray areas that you feel are detrimental, but another Christian doesn't? (example: music, TV, substances)
6. Being tempted is not a sin, but do you ever find yourself entertaining the temptation?
7. Have you ever thought about how fine Potiphar's wife may have been?! (or ladies, how fine some of those Biblical hunks must have been?!) Would you have been able to resist this kind of constant seduction? Why or why not?
8. Discuss Matthew 15:11 (key verse). In what ways have you heard it discussed? Could it be taken out of context?

Ask if anyone has any additional thoughts before closing.

# CHAPTER 17: NO REGRETS

This chapter focuses on our conflicted desire to serve self and God. We regret that if we indulge in sin, we're failing to strengthen our spirit and vice versa (because if we indulge in the spirit, we're neglecting the desires of the flesh).

I discuss the possibility of having bucket list items, or things we would like to do or experience before giving ourselves completely to God. But the truth is, the desires of the flesh are insatiable. Despite knowing this, we still try to gain carnal satisfaction.

Ultimately, only death to self can produce a dramatic change in our lives, giving God the glory. Failing to die to self will keep us from our main purpose as Christians, which is to produce other Christians. We remain a 'single seed.'

**KEY VERSE:** "'And what does pleasure accomplish?' I tried cheering myself with wine, and embracing folly—my mind still guiding me with wisdom. I wanted to see what was good for people to do under the heavens during the few days of their lives." Ecclesiastes 2:2-3

1. Do you have a bucket list of things you would like to do or experience before giving yourself completely to God? Share some items.
2. Do you ever feel like you're missing out on things because of your faith?
3. In what ways do you try to simultaneously appease both your flesh and spirit? (Give examples).
4. Do you think you would be comfortable with 'dying to your flesh' after enjoying certain pleasures?
5. Discuss Ecclesiastes 2:2-3 (key verse). If the desires of the flesh are insatiable, why do we keep trying to satisfy them?

6. Despite King Solomon's wisdom, he tried to satisfy his flesh. Why?
7. Do we take responsibility to draw people to Christ, or do we leave it up to the pastor? Elaborate.
8. Do we view bringing people to Christ as more of an elective than an ultimate purpose?
9. Discuss John 12:24: "Very truly I tell you, unless a kernel of wheat falls to the ground and dies, it remains only a single seed. But if it dies, it produces many seeds."

Ask if anyone has any additional thoughts before closing.

# CHAPTER 18: PRODIGAL PROSPECTS

The chapter begins by addressing how much we appreciate crazy testimonies and overlook the testimonies of those who haven't gone through any major rebellion. There's a certain mystique about learning for yourself, and coming to God after having all your fun.

Like the prodigal son, we make indulgence our focus, but don't realize our folly until some hard moment comes along. It is then when we reach out to our forgotten God.

In the section *First Words*, I discuss the *Parable of the Talents*, which compares our lives to servants who have been given gold; in our case, gifts to invest.

**KEY VERSE:** "Whoever tries to keep their life will lose it, and whoever loses their life will preserve it." Luke 17:33

1. What is the craziest testimony you have ever heard?
2. Have you ever been jealous of the fun someone had in his or her past?
3. The author talks about how eating steak made him feel like "this is what life is about." Do you sometimes make the same mistake—making your life's purpose the indulgence of the senses?
4. The author calls grace a cornerstone and a stumbling stone. Discuss.
5. Discuss Luke 17:33 (key verse).
6. Do you recognize your life as a resource from God that is meant to be managed, or do you take ownership of your life?
7. How has taking ownership of your life made it difficult to serve or submit to God?

8. Do you feel like God should take notice when you do things for Him? Do you try to remind Him? Give examples.
9. Do you feel like God has or hasn't given you much to invest for the kingdom? What have you have been given? Have you utilized it? If not, why or why not?
10. If you haven't gone through any major rebellious period, how do you avoiding being like the prideful or grumbling 'good son'? Why is it easy to fall into a trap of thinking you are better or more deserving of God's love? Why is that thinking so dangerous?
11. How does being like the 'good son' strain your relationship with the 'prodigal son' and the Father?

Ask if anyone has any additional thoughts before closing.

# CHAPTER 19: GET RIGHTEOUS OR DIE TRYING

The Pharisees hoped to trap Jesus with a question, asking Him whether it was right to pay taxes to Caesar or not. The reason this was such a crucial question was because of our attachment to money. We obsess about it, work hard for it, it means everything to us... but to Jesus, it wasn't very important.

Just as Caesar's image is what gave the money value, God's image upon us gives us value. The source of our value and meaningfulness is rooted in God and finding our way back to Him through Jesus, our mediator. But somehow, we often overlook this ultimate purpose and focus on secondary things like work, relationships, etc.

Despite knowing that money cannot buy happiness, we still seek it. Our earthly desires are insatiable—it is impossible to satisfy them—and King Solomon advised us not to make the same mistake he did.

Ultimately, we are urged to purse joy over happiness.

**KEY VERSE:** "But seek first his kingdom and his righteousness, and all these things will be given to you as well." Matthew 6:33

1. What are some things you feel will give your life purpose, aside from God? Do those things ever eclipse your actual purpose in God?
2. In the section, *House Rules*, the author asks us, "Where exactly do our investments lie? And if, or when they fall apart, what then?" Discuss a situation in which you invested all of yourself into something that fell apart.
3. Discuss Matthew 13:44: "The kingdom of heaven is like treasure hidden in a field. When a man found it, he hid it again, and then in his joy went and sold all he had and bought that field." Are you like the man in the parable, or

are you reluctant to give up your kingdom for God's? Why?

4. Discuss Ecclesiastes 5:10: "Whoever loves money never has enough; whoever loves wealth is never satisfied with their income. This too is meaningless." Why is it so easy to be obsessed with money?

5. What does it mean to exhaust pleasure? Have you ever exhausted pleasure? Elaborate.

6. We've all experienced happiness, but do you have joy? If so, how has it helped you get through difficult times?

Ask if anyone has any additional thoughts before closing.

# CHAPTER 20: LOSING PURPOSE

The chapter begins by discussing our desire to be called "good and faithful servants" despite failing to be good or faithful. There are billions of 'Christians' in the world, and this should have resulted in the world's transformation. However, many of us are Christian by name only.

In the section *Selling Jesus*, witnessing styles are broken up into three categories: the cold-caller, the counter-rep, and the in-store representative. People don't want to be sold Jesus; most likely, they already know about Him. What they need is to see the value in following Jesus—it must be obvious, meaningful, and productive.

In the section *The Mission Statement*, we are reminded that Jesus had a clear mission for His life, and as His followers, our lives' missions must be modeled after His. Otherwise, we will be using a vague framework to guide us... ultimately dwindling into becoming a 'regular Christians.'

**KEY VERSE:** "And whatever you do, whether in word or deed, do it all in the name of the Lord Jesus, giving thanks to God the Father through him." Colossians 3:17

1. What is the comfort in being a Christian in name only?
2. Do people view Christians who share their faith to be like salesmen? Why?
3. Have you ever witnessed to people? If so, give examples.
4. Do you ever fall into the three categories of selling Jesus: cold-caller, counter-rep, in-store rep? Elaborate.
5. Has anyone ever tried to sell you on something that clearly wasn't working for them, like a skin cream or diet pill? If so, how did you react?
6. Is Christ's value in your life obvious to others? From their perspective, is Jesus working out for you?

7. How would you practically apply Jesus's mission statement to your life?
8. What differentiates your life from that of generally good people?
9. Do you ever see yourself as a 'regular Christian?' How can this mindset cripple your ability to become an effective Christian?
10. Do you attack or bind Satanic strongholds? What does that entail?

Ask if anyone has any additional thoughts before closing.

# CHAPTER 21: PROCESSED CHRISTIANITY

In this chapter, I discuss how the food processing industry has lowered the quality of our food to be cheaper and more appealing, while robbing us of wholeness. This is similar to the way good things in life are exchanged for unequal or harmful counterparts. For example, love is often exchanged for lust.

Mainstream Christianity has become processed to appeal to the masses—our numbers peak as the cost of being a follower of Christ plummets. It has done three things: 1) modified the makeup of a disciple (it no longer requires discipline) 2) sweetened difficult teachings and polarizing beliefs, and 3) recovered scraps of Christian consciousness. Just like processed fast foods, our processed, comfortable faith cannot be taken seriously.

Like organic options, the cost of truly following Jesus may seem to some as impractical.

**KEY VERSE:** "Then Jesus said to his disciples, 'Whoever wants to be my disciple must deny themselves and take up their cross and follow me.'" Matthew 16:24

1. In what ways has Christianity become processed to fit people's lifestyles, both presently and throughout history?
2. How do 'sweetened teachings' hurt the faith?
3. Processed teaching creates processed Christians. Would you consider yourself to be processed or organic? Why?
4. Discuss Matthew 8:20: "Jesus replied, 'Foxes have dens and birds have nests, but the Son of Man has no place to lay his head.'" Why wouldn't Jesus allow some people to follow Him?
5. Jesus said, 'If you hold to my teaching, you are really my disciples.' Do you hold all of His teachings, or do you take comfort in holding just some of His teachings?

Ask if anyone has any additional thoughts before closing.

# A MODEST PROPOSAL TO END CHURCH CLOSURE

In this letter, I cited what seems like an epidemic—the plight of the modern church. I offered suggestions on how to stay hip and modern to reach the youth. But then in a quick change of fortunes, I cite the church's ability to leverage real estate to boost its own profitability—leasing out space to other businesses even if they stand for things that go against Christian principles.

Once we're brought to reject the proposal—because of the glaring conflict of interest—we're reminded how we, the true temples of God, give ourselves to other conflicting uses as well. Ultimately, it would be better if our buildings are compromised, but not our character.

**KEY VERSE:** "Don't you know that you yourselves are God's temple and that God's Spirit dwells in your midst?" 1 Corinthians 3:16

1. Do churches need cool youth pastors? Is the youth pastor at your church cool?
2. Why do you think kids are leaving the church? Is it a seasonal rebellion, or does it look more permanent?
3. How have the media (music, television, etc.), miseducation, and hypocrisy shaped people's opinions of the church?
4. Discuss the detrimental effects (to yourself and others) of being a 'compromised' temple.
5. Discuss 1 Corinthians 3:16 (key verse).

Ask if anyone has any additional thoughts before closing.

# CHAPTER 22: SCREENED BY THE SCREENS

In this chapter, I begin with discussing our fixation on things with screens—cell phones, laptops, television, movies. Often times, we are so distracted by these things—they waste huge sums of time, but we refuse to correct ourselves. Distraction is a tool of the devil, and he has a distraction for all of us... Oftentimes, we fall for the same distraction over and over. It is important to understand your distraction, how and when it comes, and in what ways you can overcome it.

In *The Big Three,* I discussed the three main things that encompass worldliness: the lust of the flesh, the lust of the eyes, and the pride of life.

In *Indulging in The Spirit,* I discussed the often overlooked practice of fasting and prayer—which targets our greatest material desire, food.

Ultimately, we must be aware of our screens/distractions, because the enemy uses them to make us lose sight of our purpose, and reinforces unbelievers' purpose.

**KEY VERSE:** "For everything in the world – the lust of the flesh, the lust of the eyes, and the pride of life – comes not from the Father but from the world. The world and its desires pass away, but whoever does the will of God lives forever." 1 John 2:16

1. How often do you look at your phone? How does it affect your productivity and your spiritual life?
2. Have you ever fasted from social media? What prompted you to do so, how long did you last, and what did you gain or learn?
3. The author likens the devil's tactic to distract us to a pick-n-roll... one we keep falling for. What are some screens in your life, and in what ways can you overcome them? Can you do it on your own? If not, have you asked for help?

4. We cannot simultaneously satisfy both worldly and spiritual urges without them adversely affecting the other. Give an example of how a desire to please either spirit or flesh affected the other?

5. Do you take time to pray, or do you replace prayer by sending God little messages here and there? If so, what are those 'little messages' about?

6. How does sending God little messages (in place of prayer) affect your relationship with Him?

7. Have you ever fasted? If so, what did you gain from it?

8. Jesus told the crowds that they were only looking for Him because He gave them loaves and fish (John 6:26). He knew that their indulgence was not for His word, but for physical satisfaction. How can we be sure that we are seeking Jesus with the right motive?

9. Isn't it amazing that King David was considered a 'man after God's own heart' despite his major sins? Discuss how this relates to us.

10. Based on the section *The Pity Party,* how can getting distracted or losing our purpose in Christ reinforce an unbeliever's secular purpose? Have you ever reinforced an unbeliever's secular purpose? Give examples.

Ask if anyone has any additional thoughts before closing.

# CHAPTER 23: ONLY GOD CAN JUDGE ME

This chapter begins by discussing the overuse of the adage, "Only God can judge me." We often think of it as a way of relieving ourselves of liability before men, but Apostle Paul told us about his desire to be innocent before both God and man.

It briefly goes over Paul's trial and how we may not easily persuade someone to be a Christian, but we can easily persuade them not to be.

**KEY VERSE:** "So I strive always to keep my conscience clear before God and man." Acts 24:16

1. Have you ever used the 'Only God can judge me' defense? Why, and what did it do for you?
2. Do you suppress the thought of Judgment Day? Why, or why not? What are your thoughts on it?
3. What is the importance of being innocent before both God and men? How can it become a great witness for your faith?
4. Have you ever had an interaction with someone—either positive or negative—that may have affected how that person viewed Christianity?
5. Have you ever thought of the possibility that you could be committing a sin at the Hour of the Lord's return?
6. Can you identify with Kendrick Lamar's lyric, "I am a sinner, who's probably gonna sin again, Lord forgive me." How can, or has that led to a relaxed attitude towards sin?
7. Have you ever asked God to forgive you for something so many times that you stopped asking for grace? How do you get out of that cycle? Why is it so dangerous?

Ask if anyone has any additional thoughts before closing.

# CHAPTER 24: BEYOND UNREASONABLE DOUBT

This chapter begins by discussing the possibility of comfortable Christians' punishment on Judgment Day being worse than that of non-believers. In this case, God's existence would actually be a detriment to us. Like many who are becoming agnostic, we too have our doubts.

In *Reference Points*, I discussed how crippling doubt can be, and how doubt can overcome us just as it overcame the Israelites, despite having their 'reference points.'

As the chapter continues, I glanced at the 'problem of evil' and how deceptive it is to 'lean on our own mis-understanding'. I also discussed Jesus's claims and Pilate's retort. Although people may not find any wrong in Jesus, like Pilate, they decide within their hearts that the 'truth' is either relative or cannot be known.

In the section *Amazing Faith,* I discussed the centurion's request for his servant to be healed, and the doubts of the disciples.

**KEY VERSE:** "Trust in the Lord with all your heart and lean not on your own understanding; in all your ways submit to him, and he will make your paths straight." Proverbs 3:5-6

1. Would a Comfortable Christian really be worse off than an unbeliever on Judgment Day?
2. How has increasing agnosticism and atheism affected you? (in terms of friends, media, society, government, etc.)
3. Isn't it amazing that the Israelites could doubt God after witnessing so many miracles? Has God ever done anything miraculous in your life? Have you ever doubted God in spite of that?
4. Why is it so easy to forget these reference points?
5. Have you ever been crippled by doubt? If so, how did you overcome it?
6. Why is it tempting to compare our sins to others?

7. Discuss the atheist girl who prayed to get out of a court fine in the section *Lean On Your Own Misunderstanding*. Why is it so easy to call things coincidences? What does it say about our ability to unreasonably doubt everything?

8. Discuss G.K. Chesterton's quote:

> "But the new rebel is a skeptic, and will not entirely trust anything. He has no loyalty; therefore he can never be really a revolutionist. And the fact that he doubts everything really gets in his way when he wants to denounce anything. For all denunciation implies a moral doctrine of some kind; and the modern revolutionist doubts not only the institution he denounces, but the doctrine by which he denounces it. . . . As a politician, he will cry out that war is a waste of life, and then, as a philosopher, that all life is waste of time. A Russian pessimist will denounce a policeman for killing a peasant, and then prove by the highest philosophical principles that the peasant ought to have killed himself. . . . The man of this school goes first to a political meeting, where he complains that savages are treated as if they were beasts; then he takes his hat and umbrella and goes on to a scientific meeting, where he proves that they practically are beasts. In short, the modern revolutionist, being an infinite skeptic, is always engaged in undermining his own mines. In his book on politics he attacks men for trampling on morality; in his book on ethics he attacks morality for trampling on men. Therefore the modern man in revolt has become practically useless for all purposes of revolt. By rebelling against everything he has lost his right to rebel against anything."

Ask if anyone has any additional thoughts before closing.

# CHAPTER 25: SAY YO' PRAYERS SUCKA

I began the chapter by chuckling at the idea of saying an emergency repentance prayer as our demise swiftly approaches. We often put off repentance for a later date, as if there is something to gain by barely squeaking into the kingdom.

Later I discussed our worry about some catastrophe or apocalyptic event ending the world while overlooking the fact that our lives could end at any time.

In the section *Neglected by the Neglected*, I discussed the *Parable of the Banquet* and how pre-occupation can keep us from pursuing God.

Then I shared a story about a handicapped man who didn't want my 'sympathy' despite being danger and how this relates to our relationship with Jesus.

Finally, I discussed the structures in our lives in which our faith lies—wealth, health, relationships.

**KEY VERSE:** "Moreover, no one knows when their hour will come: As fish are caught in a cruel net, or birds are taken in a snare, so people are trapped by evil times that fall unexpectedly upon them." Ecclesiastes 9:12

1. Have you ever said a prayer of repentance because you thought your life was in danger?
2. Are people reluctant to repent while they are young because they think they have time to do that later? Why do we expect to live long?
3. How would we practice faith if death was imminent? (For example, if we were in the military fighting, lived in war-torn regions, etc.)
4. Discuss the *Parable of the Workers in the Vineyard* (Matthew 20). Which worker do you identify with?

5. Discuss the *Parable of the Banquet* (Luke 14). What things, even if good and noble, are pre-occupying you from God's invitation?

6. Have ever found yourself in a cycle of re-dedication to Christ? What is pulling you away? Do you feel like your lack of growth is frustrating to God?

7. How can you be certain that your repentance is genuine?

Ask if anyone has any additional thoughts before closing.

# CHAPTER 26: IDENTITY THEFT

This chapter begins with an analogy of our new identity in Christ being like that of a criminal who escapes jurisdiction with a new identity—only able to be caught if he or she returns.

The chapter continues by discussing the importance of understanding the devil's schemes to steal our identity in Christ. The author references C.S. Lewis's book, *Screwtape Letters*—a book about a senior level demon advising his nephew demon who has just been assigned to regain the soul of a new convert.

In the section *Zero Liability*, we discuss our attitudes towards sin—oftentimes being relaxed with little emphasis on discipline—and the thin line between needing grace and abusing it.

**KEY VERSE:** "What shall we say, then? Shall we go on sinning so that grace may increase?" Romans 6:1

1. Do you see yourself as the Righteousness of Christ? If not, why not?
2. Have you ever been a victim of identity theft? If so, elaborate.
3. Discuss the three types of schemes of the devil (phishing, void value, imitation). How have you guarded yourself from these three schemes? How have you fallen for them in the past?
4. Discuss the Full Armor of God (Ephesians 6:10-20). Do you have it on?
5. Do you have a sense of urgency to repent when you're outside of God's will? Or do you figure you'll find your way back eventually?
6. Have you read *Screwtape Letters*? If so, what practical/relatable points would you like to share from it?
7. What is the difference between abusing grace and struggling with a sin?

Ask if anyone has any additional thoughts before closing.

# CHAPTER 27: THE UNGRATEFUL DEAD

The chapter begins with the concept that we are only grateful for things once they are gone—whether it be a relationship, a job, or an opportunity, we realize what we had after it is too late to express our gratitude. At that time, appreciation is pointless. Likewise, our appreciation for the cross would be pointless if we missed the opportunity to be genuine followers.

Then I discussed hell, and Christ's separation from the Father when He bore our sin.

The section *Is Ignorance Bliss or Miss?* discussed our inability to miss something we never had. Since we've never had an unhampered, direct connection with God, it can be difficult to long for it.

The section *Shame On Me* discussed my worry that my Comfortable Christian lifestyle has brought shame to Jesus. Then in the section *I Never Knew You*, I discussed the possibility of Jesus saying those dreaded words and what our responses would to that would be.

**KEY VERSE:** "Whoever says, 'I know Him,' but does not do what He commands is a liar, and the truth is not in that person." 1 John 2:4

1. Why does it often take loss to appreciate something or someone?
2. What are some things or people that you regret not appreciating when you had the opportunity? Has that regret made you appreciative or bitter?
3. Discuss your understanding of hell. Do you avoid thinking about it? Do you see hell as a separation from God and things of God (like common, good nature), or just as a fiery punishment?

4. We often casually say, "Jesus died for our sins," or "Jesus became sin for us," but do we think about what it was like for Jesus to be separated from the Father?
5. Have you ever been 'ashamed of the gospel?' If so, when and why? How can we become bold for Christ?
6. Discuss 1 John 2:4 (key verse). Why is it hard to see that the "truth is not in us?"
7. Have you ever thought about what it would be like to be told, 'I never knew you?' Would you still like Jesus and appreciate His sacrifice afterwards, or would you become bitter?

Ask if anyone has any additional thoughts before closing.

## CHEERS! TO ALL OF THE PASTORS

This letter begins by applauding leaders who allow us to forget that being a Christian is about discipleship and instead focus our attention on prosperity and grace. It gives the pastors the benefit of the doubt—because we may not have listened to them anyway, which somewhat justifies their ultra-soft approach.

The letter does, however, seem displeased with the pastors for emphasizing discipline when it comes to tithes and offering—and expresses suspicion of the luxurious lifestyle some of them live.

**KEY VERSE:** "For the time will come when people will not put up with sound doctrine. Instead, to suit their own desires, they will gather around them a great number of teachers to say what their itching ears want to hear." 2 Timothy 4:3

1. What are your thoughts on churches that are focused on prosperity or grace? Are they overlooking discipline?
2. The letter says, "Whatever our ages, we have remained infants in Christ — sustained only by your regurgitation of the Word." Why is this problematic?
3. Can prosperity gospel pastors still be used by God to bring in the lost?
4. Do you think pastors should be very wealthy? Why or why not?
5. Do you think false ministers are aware that they are false ministers? (I am not referring to blatantly false prophets who fabricate things)
6. Have you ever been attracted to teachings 'that your itching ears want to hear?' How did you recognize that it was wrong?

Ask if anyone has any additional thoughts before closing.

# CHAPTER 28: ELEMENTARY, MY DEAR

In this chapter, I shared my experience with my newborn son, to whom I am both a father and a comforter. I dream of nurturing him to an age until he is capable of becoming a father and comforter. Likewise, our Father seeks to see us mature, but we often remain as infants in Christ.

The section *Superficial Maturity* discussed how we often deceive ourselves by thinking we are spiritually maturing. Even our desire to spiritually mature comes into question.

The sections *Deadbeat Losers* and *Stakeholders* considered the believer who never spiritually matures. *Know Yo' Role* discussed how all who are in the Body of Christ have roles and responsibilities that edify each other—and we focus on the role of being an encourager. The section *Bulding Block-ades* discussed serving wholeheartedly.

Finally, the section *Prey or Predator* considered how every animal, no matter how fearsome, is vulnerable at infancy. Likewise, we, the children of God, will always be prone to the devil's attacks unless we mature spiritually—and ultimately attack the devil.

**KEY VERSE:** "Brothers and sisters, I could not address you as people who live by the Spirit but as people who are still worldly—mere infants in Christ." 1 Corinthians 3:1

1. How long have you been a Christian? Have you matured or remained stagnant?
2. Do you really want to spiritually mature, or do you just like being motivated by good messages? How can you tell the difference?
3. We often assume that our worship leaders or speakers have spiritually matured. The author gives an example how, although he was not necessarily maturing, he was

getting praise for giving good messages. How can than this be a stumbling stone for leaders?

4. Have you ever been in a place of leadership, but inside, you were far from God?

5. Why do we feel the urgency to mature physically but not spiritually?

6. What affect does it have on the church when everyone remains an infant in Christ? What effect does it have on the leaders?

7. In John 15, Jesus says that branches that do not remain in Him are cut off and thrown into a fire. Do we take this warning seriously? If not, why?

8. Do you feel like you don't have a role in the Body of Christ? Elaborate.

9. 1 Corinthians 12 says, "Those parts of the body that seem to be weaker are indispensable." Have you overlooked your ability or responsibility to be an encourager? In what ways can you encourage and edify others?

10. Discuss Ephesians 6:7-8: "Serve wholeheartedly, as if you were serving the Lord, not people, because you know that the Lord will reward each one for whatever good they do." Why do we feel the need to be rewarded when we serve?

11. Do you ever ask God to guide your life even though you haven't allowed Him to guide your day? Why do we overlook that?

12. How has remaining an 'infant in Christ' made you an easy target for the enemy?

13. Do you ever see yourself maturing to the point where you target the devil's works? If not, why?

Ask if anyone has any additional thoughts before closing.

# CHAPTER 29: GUILTY CONSCIENCE

This chapter begins with a quote about repentance from C.S. Lewis and a discussion of the difference between two types of guilt: godly sorrow and condemnation. Godly sorrow is a good, and it brings us closer to God; meanwhile, condemnation keeps us away. Two great examples of godly sorrow and condemnation in action are seen in the stories of Peter and Judas.

The section *Clearing Your Conscience* discusses God's desire to free us from not just the penalty of our sin, but to see ourselves as His righteousness—anything less is undermining Christ's sacrifice.

The section *Save Your Apologies* discussed the types of apologies that we make when we repent.

**KEY VERSE:** "How much more, then, will the blood of Christ, who through the eternal Spirit offered himself unblemished to God, cleanse our conscience from acts that lead to death, so that we may serve the living God?" Hebrews 9:14

1. Do you ever feel guilty despite the fact that you are forgiven? How can that hurt you?
2. Have you ever been forgiven for betraying a friend, yet you couldn't forgive yourself? How did that strain the relationship?
3. Have you ever come to church after a wild night or after committing a sin? Did that experience harden your heart or soften it?
4. Why are we so afraid of being seen as hypocrites? Does it have anything to do with how quick we are to judge others?
5. Is there a re-occurring sin in your life? What kind of apology have you offered: "Sorry I offended you" or "sorry for my action"?

6.  Do you hate your sin, or do you hate having to apologize for it?

Ask if anyone has any additional thoughts before closing.

# CHAPTER 30: ACCEPTING ADDICTION

This chapter discussed how we may not really want to be free from our addictions. The chapter also looked at the environmental hazards and our futile attempts to break free.

In the section *Freedom Façade*, I likened our 'freedom from sin' to the emancipation of the slaves after the Civil War. Sure, they were free, but many had no choice but to stay on plantations and work as sharecroppers—virtually the same as being a slave. Likewise, many of us Christians are only free in name, but not in action.

The section *Accountability Counts* discussed the importance of strengthening each other in areas where we are weak. I also wrote about the three fears that stop us from opening up to other believers about an addiction.

The section *Intimacy Issues* discussed how the main problem with our relationship with God is that we don't draw near to Him. I also reviewed how 'resisting the devil and he will flee' only comes after first 'submitting to God.'

**KEY VERSE:** "Submit yourselves to God, resist the devil, and he will flee from you." James 4:7

1. What are some common yet embarrassing addictions?
2. Have you ever come to a point when you realized, "Whoa, I am addicted to this," and what did you do about it?
3. Have you ever failed so many times in overcoming an addiction that you just stopped trying? How did that affect your spiritual life?
4. Have you ever been set free from something for a considerable amount of time, only to fall back into addiction? Why, and what happened? How can you avoid that in the future?

5. Have you ever used the Word to thwart temptation? If so, what verses have you used?

6. Which of the three major fears has stopped you from asking someone to keep you accountable? (the fear of gossip, the fear of being identified by the addiction, the fear of actually become free)

7. Has anyone ever asked you to keep them accountable? If so, how did you go about it?

8. Do we often focus too hard on eliminating our addictions on our own instead of allowing those chains to break off as a result of 'drawing near to God'? Elaborate.

9. What does it mean to 'submit yourselves to God' before 'resisting the devil'? Why is that so important? Have you done so?

Ask if anyone has any additional thoughts before closing.

# CHAPTER 31: I AM THE LIMIT

This chapter begins by discussing God's desire to empower us with the Holy Spirit, making the 'sky the limit.' But on the other hand, our flesh seeks to make 'I' the limit. The flesh is fine with church attendance, prayer, etc., but its main focus is repressing our transformation.

The section *The Comfortable Christian Manifesto* discussed our bi-partisan approach to fulfilling the desires of the flesh and spirit. Although this approach leads to deadlock, it is still ideal for the flesh (better than its outright crucifixion).

The section *Mission Unaccomplished* discussed understanding who our enemy is—self. We cannot blame our spiritual failure on others or on the devil; we must understand that it is our own flesh standing in our way. And victory isn't usually a one-hitter-quitter, but more about winning the little battles, day by day.

The section *An 'F' for Effort* discussed not wanting to commit sin versus not wanting sin. We often spend so much energy trying to correct our sin instead of allowing God to transform our desires—a change that only comes about by God increasing and our decreasing.

The section *Clearance Through Perseverance* discussed the importance of wrestling the flesh, even when we lose. We are also reminded not to set limits on what the Holy Spirit can purge from us. We often hope that God not only forgives our inability, but also our willingness to persevere.

The section, *The Fresh Odor* offers a warning not to take pride in our righteousness. Otherwise, we become as foul as the Pharisees. And finally, the section *Long Live the King* discusses the need to not just gain control but keep control because the flesh is always seeking to resurge.

**KEY VERSE:** "He must increase, but I must decrease." John 3:30

1.  What things do we blame for our lack of spiritual maturity? How can deferring blame prevent us from seeing that our flesh is the enemy? Give an example.
2.  How can you tell if your flesh is dictating your prayers? What do you usually pray for when it is?
3.  Have you ever tried to allow God to increase in your life without you decreasing? Elaborate.
4.  Do you feel like you have to be perfect to glorify God? In what ways can God be glorified in your weaknesses?
5.  Do you ever feel like the lion who ordered the 'safari salad' in the section *An 'F' for Effort*? Elaborate.
6.  Have you ever limited how much the Holy Spirit can convict you? (like the story in *Clearance Through Perseverance*). What are some things you're not allowing God to touch?
7.  Have you ever fallen into pride because you were being good or overcoming something for an extended period of time? Why is that dangerous?
8.  2 Corinthians 10 tells us to "take captive every thought to make it obedient to Christ." What does this entail? Have you done this? Why or why not?
9.  How can we stay vigilant against the flesh once we've overcome it?

Ask if anyone has any additional thoughts before closing.

# CHAPTER 32: UNDER THE INSPIRATION

The chapter began by discussing our desire to be inspired and the difference between inspiration and influence. We love to get inspired by God but rarely do we let Him influence every aspect of our lives.

The section *Under Old Management* discussed how we are inspired by church on Sunday, but it doesn't continue on throughout our week. Ultimately, we become hearers of the Word but not doers.

The section *Epic Fail* discussed the dynamic of a pre-battle speech, which although is very inspiring, in this scenario, no one acts. In fact, our inaction may prevent others from acting.

The section *Dedication to Inspiration* discusses how our dedication may not be to God but to repeated inspiration. Like a car with a bad battery, we constantly need a jump. We often spend our whole lives trying to get the inspiration instead of giving the inspiration.

The section *Supplement Diet* discusses how foolish it would be to use supplements and vitamins without a proper diet. This is exactly what it is like to depend on sermons, worship, etc. We are trying to survive off of God's inspiration and not His influence—not daily bread.

**KEY VERSE:** "Do not merely listen to the word, and so deceive yourselves. Do what it says." James 1:22

1. What is the difference between being inspired by alcohol versus being under the influence of alcohol? How does that correlate with being God-inspired versus God-influenced?
2. In what ways can you lose your appeal to others by being 'God influenced?'

3. Jesus said, "If the world hates you, keep in mind that it hated me first. If you belonged to the world, it would love you as its own ... A servant is not greater than his master. If they persecuted me, they will persecute you also." Have you ever been scorned, mocked, or hated for your faith? If so, did that discourage or encourage you?

4. Why is the approval of our friends (who come and go) so important, especially in the teen years? How can one become bold for Christ during this time?

5. Discuss James 1:22 (key verse).

6. Are you a hearer or a doer of the Word? If a hearer, why? If a doer, were you always a doer, or did you make a change?

7. In what ways do hearers prevent others from being doers?

8. Have you ever tried becoming the inspiration instead of only seeking inspiration? If so, elaborate. If not, why not?

9. Do you 'supplement' your walk with God yet overlook the importance of 'daily bread'? Elaborate.

10. Has that supplementing led to frustrating highs and lows in your walk? How so?

Ask if anyone has any additional thoughts before closing.

# CHAPTER 33: SEPARATION OF CHURCH... AND STATE OF MIND

This final chapter begins by asking the reader to identify the things he or she struggles with, and to question whether we are unable or unwilling to change.

The chapter continues by discussing that, despite being told as children that we are unique and can do anything, many of us end up conforming to our environments. True uniqueness and greatness isn't a birthright; it's in our ability to transform.

In the section *Pending Metamorphosis*, I liken a Christian who has only half-changed to a caterpillar that only partly turns into a butterfly—unable to operate in neither the old life nor the new life.

The section *Missing Your Vision* and *Erasing the Pentecost* discusses how important it is to allow the Holy Spirit to empower us to carry out God's will—to be renewed and transformed by His spirit. Even the disciples were unable to carry out God's will before the Spirit came upon them. So how much more do we, who haven't witnessed Christ in the flesh, need His empowerment? The Holy Spirit was the difference between the disciples being inspired by Jesus' teaching, parables, and miracles, and being able to step into their call.

Ultimately, the Spirit reveals the spiritual warfare around us and how the devil seeks to keep us as Comfortable Christians. We end up as Christians without the empowerment of the Christ's spirit—having the form of godliness but denying its power.

**KEY VERSE:** "Not that I have already obtained all this, or have already arrived at my goal, but I press on to take hold of that for which Christ Jesus took hold of me. Brothers and sisters, I do not consider myself yet to have taken hold of it. But one thing I do: Forgetting what is behind and straining toward what is ahead, I press on toward the goal to win the prize for which God has called me heavenward in Christ Jesus." Philippians 3:12-14

1. It's easy to point out homosexuals and what they can't change, but what is it in your life that you can't seem to change?
2. What did you dream of becoming when you were a kid? What are you now? If you've fallen short of those dreams, why?
3. Do you regard pastors or leaders as holier or greater than you are? If so, how has this attitude limited you?
4. Jesus reached us so that we can reach the world. He told us we would do greater things than Him. Why is that hard to believe?
5. Have you fallen short of your ability or calling? If so, why, and what is it?
6. Can you transform the world without being transformed yourself? Why is conforming so easy?
7. Imagine if the Holy Spirit never filled the disciples. What would have become of them? What would have become of Christianity?
8. Do believers overlook the importance of being empowered by the Holy Spirit in order to walk in victory? Elaborate.
9. What does 'being empowered' entail? How do you gain that empowerment?

Ask if anyone has any additional thoughts before closing.

## POSTSCRIPT

1. Whose plan is succeeding in your life now: God's or Satan's? Elaborate.
2. Why is keeping us content and comfortable such a useful plan for the devil?
3. In what ways may we mistake comfort as being God's plan?
4. Does Screwtape's note about repentance shock you? How can you prevent your repentance from becoming sterilized?
5. What steps will you take to break out of being a Comfortable Christian? What steps will you take to help others to break out of it?

Ask if anyone has any additional thoughts before closing.

Made in the USA
San Bernardino, CA
17 February 2020